Oxford Phonics World 3

Long Vowels

Kaj Schwermer   Julia Chang   Craig Wright

Workbook

OXFORD
UNIVERSITY PRESS

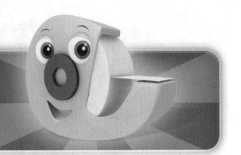

A Write and say.

a_e	tape

B Say and circle.

1.

an (ane)

2.

ape ap

3.

ane an

4.

ape ap

C Match.

1. tape •

• 2. mane

3. cape •

• 4. cane

long a

a_e

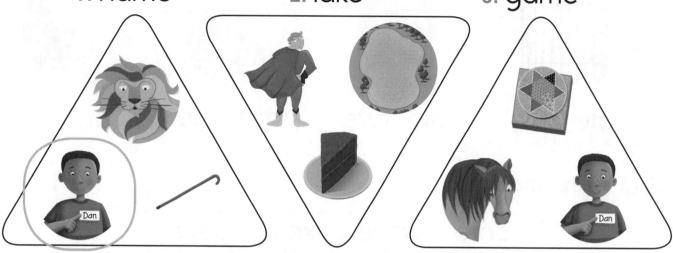

a_e **ame ake** ate ave

A Read, say, and circle.

1. name

2. lake

3. game

B Unscramble, write, and say.

1.
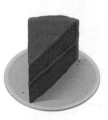
m g e a

game

2.

k c a e

3.
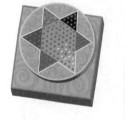
k l e a

4.

m e n a

5.

e c p a

6.

a n e c

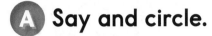

a_e ame ake **ate ave**

A Say and circle.

1.

ate   ave

2.

ate   ave

3.

ave   ate

4.

ate   ave

B Write and say.

gate   wave   ~~skate~~   cave

1.

skate

2.

3.

4.
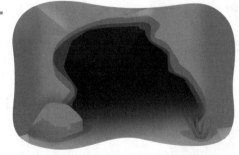

long a

ate   ave

A Find the words and underline.

dma<u>ne</u>dcakeogamefcaveqrskatefnamextwavedtapewgatejocane

B Say and circle.

1.

ake ate

2.

ape ane

3.

ave ame

4.

ate ape

C Unscramble, write, and say.

1.

t s a e k

_____

2.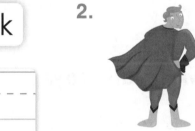

p e a c

_____

3.

p a e t

_____

4.

m n e a

Dan

_____

A Write and say.

i _ e   k t

B Match.

1.	2.	3.	4.	5.	6.
pine	ripe	pin	kite	fine	rip

C Unscramble, write, and say.

1.    e r p i

2.    t k i e

3.    e i f n

4.    n e i p

long i

i_e

A Read and check.

1.

It is a kite. ☐

It is a lime. ☑

2.

It is a bike. ☐

It is a hike. ☐

3.

What is the time? ☐

What is the lime? ☐

4.

I hike to the cave. ☐

I bike to the cave. ☐

B Write and say.

1.

i ___ e

2.

h ___ e

3.

___ i k ___

4.

t ___ e

i_e ime ike **ive ine**

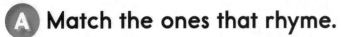

A Match the ones that rhyme.

1.
2.
3.
4.

B Write and say.

time   pine   nine   line   dive   fine

1.
2.
3.
4.
5.
6.

long i
ive   ine

A Find the words and underline.

cbikedkiteolimefpineqrlinefhikextfivedtimew

B Say, circle, and write.

1.

ine   ike

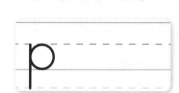
p

2.

ive   ine

f

3.

ite   ipe

k

4.

ime   ike

h

5.

ive   ime

d

6.

ite   ime

l

A Circle the ones that rhyme.

B Find, circle, and write.

c	d	q	x	d	b
n	i	a	p	s	j
k	v	l	i	m	e
l	e	i	o	a	l
c	a	n	e	u	f
h	w	e	z	p	h

1. dive

2.

3.

4.

long a

 a_e   ame   ake   ate   ave

C Do the puzzle.

1.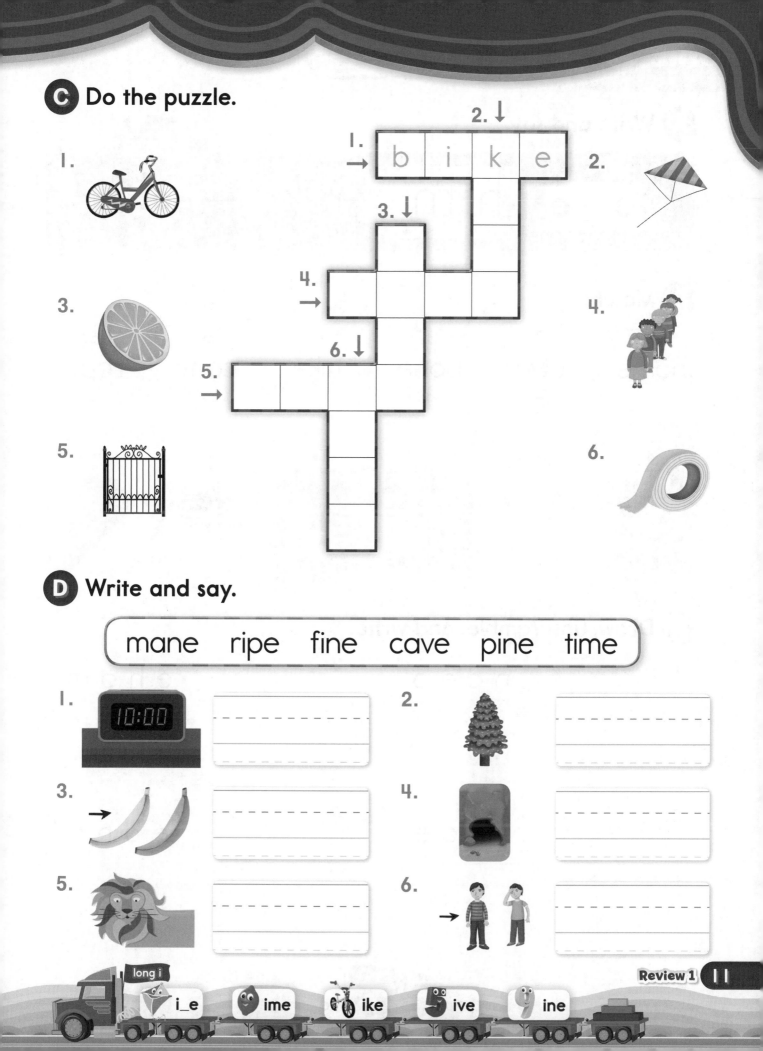

2. ↓

1. → | b | i | k | e |

2.

3. ↓

4. →

3.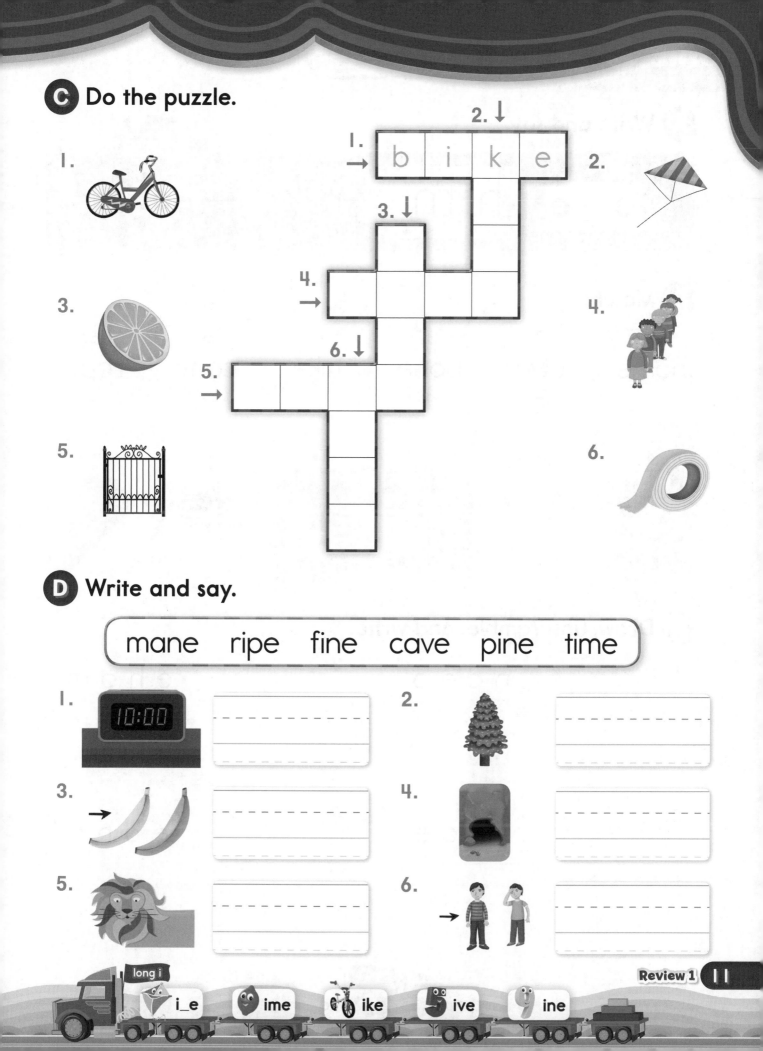

4.

6. ↓

5. →

5.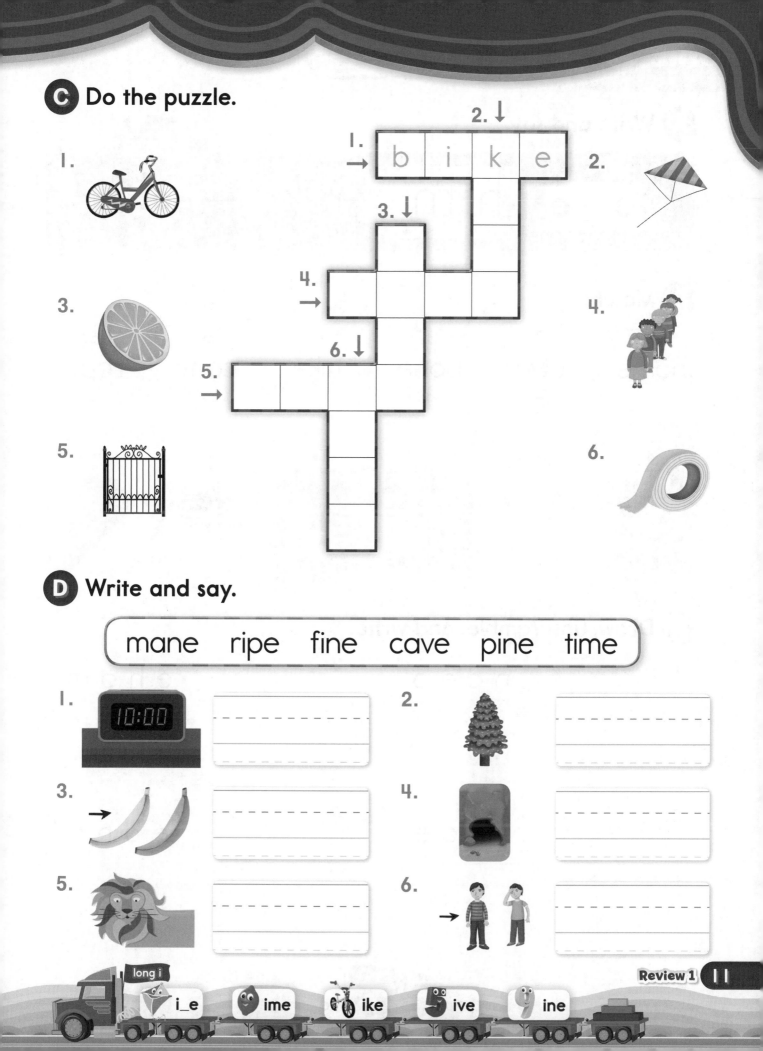

6.

D Write and say.

| mane | ripe | fine | cave | pine | time |

1.

2.

3. →

4.

5.

6. →

A Write and say.

o _ e   h m

B Match.

1.	2.	3.	4.	5.	6.
home	dive	bone	hike	cone	rope

    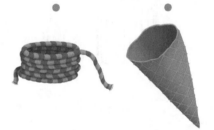

C Draw, unscramble, and write.

1.

n c e o

2.

e h o m

3.

p r o e

4.

e b n o

 long o

o_e

A Write and say.

u _ e   c b

B Match.

1. mute •         • 2. cute

3. cube •         • 4. mule

C Write and say.

cube   cute   mule   mute

1.

2.

3.

4.

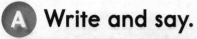

A Write and say.

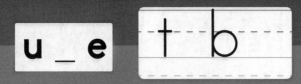

u _ e   t b

B Read and check.

1.

This is a cube. ☐
This is a tube. ☐

2.

I hum a tune. ☐
I hum a tube. ☐

3.

It is June. ☐
It is a cube. ☐

4.

This is a mule. ☐
This is a rule. ☐

C Unscramble, write, and say.

1.

n e u J

2.

e t b u

3.

n u t e

4.

u l r e

long u
u_e

A Find the words and underline.

bfhomerrconeuiJuneiwcutelomuleghtunenpropedh

B Say and circle.

1.    2.    3. 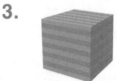   4.

u_e o_e   o_e u_e   i_e u_e   u_e a_e

C Write and say.

1.    t ___ e

2. 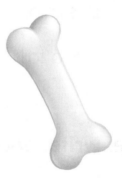   ___ o ___ e

3.    r ___ e

4.    ___ ne

 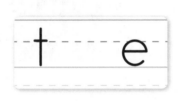

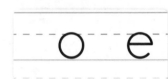

long a

ai ay

A Write and say.

 r n

B Read and check.

1.

It is rain. ☐

It is a tail. ☐

2.

It is a nail. ☐

It is a tail. ☐

3.

It is rain. ☐

It is a tail. ☐

4.

It is a gate. ☐

I wait. ☐

C Unscramble, write, and say.

1.

l i a n

_____

2.

n r i a

_____

3.

t a w i

_____

4.

a l i t

_____

long a

ai

A Write and say.

a y   b

B Read, say, and check.

1.  ay ☑ ☐

2.  ay ☐ ☐

3. 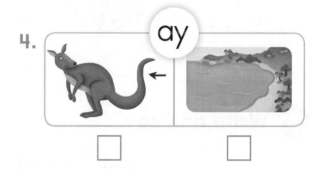 ay ☐ ☐

4. Hello! ☐ ☐

C Write and say.

1.  a

2. Hello! s

3.  y

4.  b

ai ay

A **Read, say, and circle.**

1. sail

2. mail

3. hay

4. May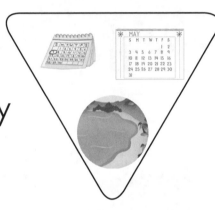

B **Write and say.**

sail   mail   hay   May

1.

2.

3.

4.

long a

ai   ay

A Find the words and underline.

wddayhlmailkhpayjuhayllMayopsailuopbayafrainw

B Say, circle, and write.

1.

ay   ai

2.

ay   ai

3.

ay   ai

4.

ay   ai

5.

ay   ai

6.

ai   ay

A Find the words and underline.

jghmulekdkhomeysutubetrqJuneoawrainpwlrulewjiwaitspp

B Do the puzzle.

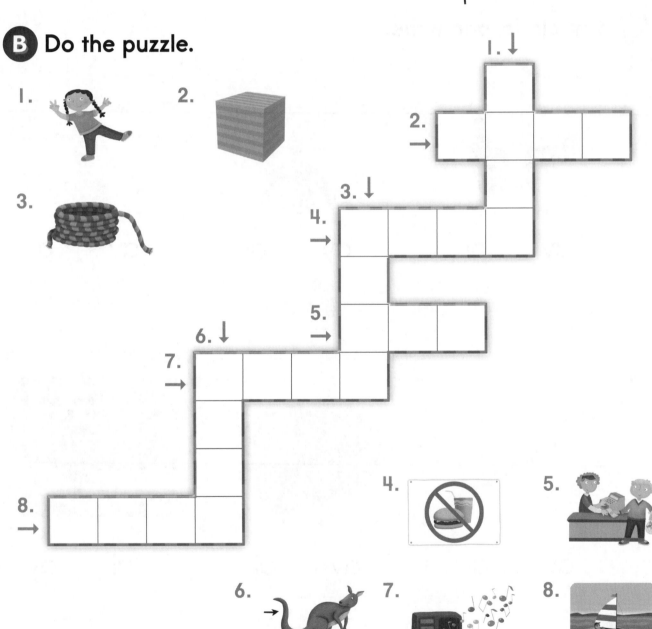

1.

2.

3.

4.

5.

6.

7.

8.

C Circle the ones that rhyme.

D Find, circle, and write.

c	o	n	e	g	h
a	k	q	s	i	u
d	i	t	a	i	l
s	p	e	y	g	k
a	m	h	l	i	c
w	a	i	t	x	z
a	k	j	r	u	s
q	b	u	p	d	h
f	w	o	t	p	j

1. _____

2. _____

3. _____

4. _____

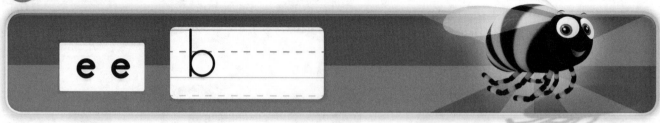

A Write and say.

e e

b

B Match.

1. bee •

 • 2. feet

3. seed •

 • 4. jeep

C Unscramble, write, and say.

1.

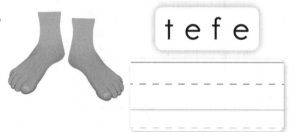

| t e f e |

2.

| d s e e |

3.

| e b e |

4.

| j p e e |

long e

ee

A Write and say.

e a | l — f |

B Match.

| 1. | 2. | 3. | 4. |
| sea | leaf | eat | meat |

C Write and say.

1.
 s

2.
 l — f

3.
 t

4.
 at

A Write and say.

y   cand

e y   k

B Say and circle.

1.   y   ey

2.   y   ey

3.   y   ey

4.   y   ey

C Read and check.

1.   I have candy. ☐
     I have a leaf. ☐

2.   It is a bee. ☐
     It is a key. ☐

3.   He is happy. ☐
     He has money. ☐

4.   I have money. ☐
     I have candy. ☐

 long e    y   ey

ee ea y ey

A Find the words and underline.

gthappyuwfeetroseedskmoneybukeywaseajhleafgh

B Say, circle, and write.

1.

ea   ee

2.

ee   y

3.

ee   ea

4.

ey   ea

C Write and say.

1.

h _ _ y

2.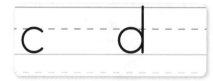

c _ _ d

3.

m _ _ t

4.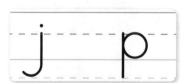

j _ _ p

A Write and say.

i g h ___ t

B Match.

1. light •

• 2. right

3. high •

• 4. night

C Unscramble, write, and say.

1.

t i g r h

_____

2.

t n g i h

_____

3.

g h i h

_____

4.

l t h i g

_____

long i

igh

A Write and say.

i e p

B Read and check.

1.
It is a die. ☐
It is a tie. ☐

2.
It is a tie. ☐
It is a light. ☐

3.
It is a pie. ☐
It is high. ☐

4.
I bike at night. ☐
I lie and wait. ☐

C Write and say.

1.
p

2.
e

3.
e

4.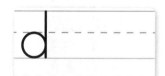
d

A Write and say.

y   sp

B Say, circle, and write.

1.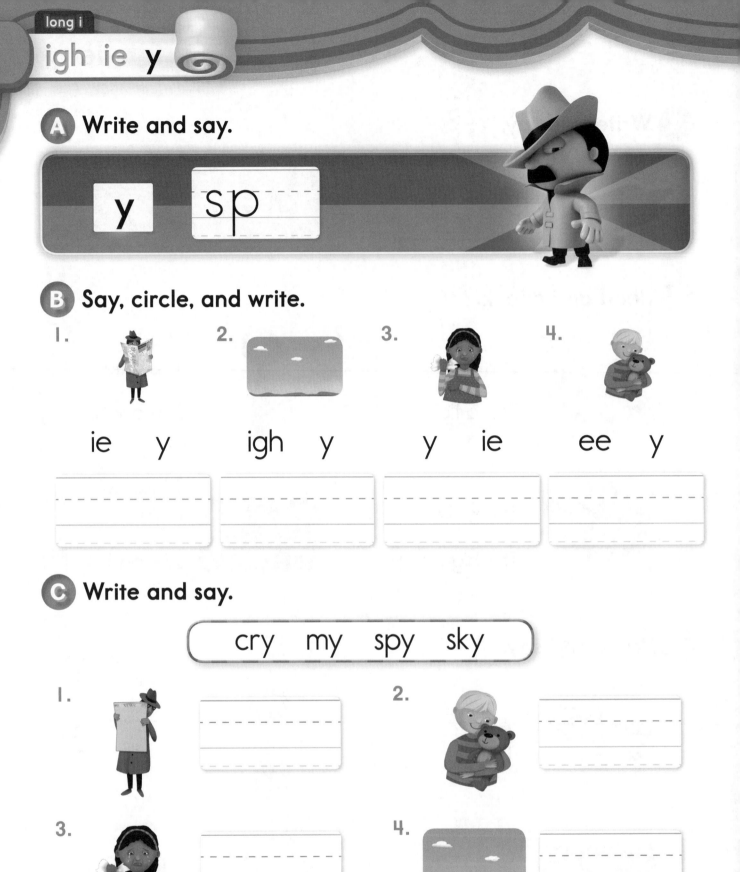

ie   y

2.

igh   y

3.

y   ie

4.

ee   y

C Write and say.

cry   my   spy   sky

1.

2.

3.

4.

long i

y

A Find the words and underline.

gnightjkhspyulightthkmylhighsyqptieqskyedieh

B Match.

1.	2.	3.	4.
ie	y	igh	ee

C Unscramble, write, and say.

1.

t r i h g

2.

y r c

3.

y s k

4.

i t e

long i   igh   ie   y

A Do the puzzle.

1.

3.

5.

7.

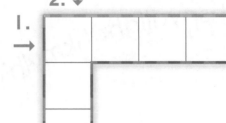

2.

4.

6.

8.

B Circle the ones that rhyme.

long e

 ee   ea   y   ey

C Write and say.

lie   candy   jeep   spy

1.

2.

3.

4.

D Find, circle, and write.

r	e	o	b	e	e
j	s	k	y	a	s
d	f	e	n	k	e
k	m	y	d	s	f
s	e	a	h	t	d
c	z	u	a	l	y

1.

2.

3.

4.

long i

 igh   ie   y

A Write and say.

o a   b _____ t

B Match.

1.	2.	3.	4.
soap	boat	coat	road

C Unscramble, write, and say.

1.

t b a o

2.

c a o t

3.

a s p o

4.

r d o a

long o
oa

A Write and say.

o w   b⎯

B Match.

1.	2.	3.	4.
yellow	bow	pillow	row

C Write and say.

1.  y⎯ll⎯

2.  b⎯

3.  ⎯⎯w

4.  pi⎯⎯w

long o

ow

A Say and check.

1.

goat

□ □ □

2.

toad

□ □ □

3.

elbow

□ □ □

4.

window

□ □ □

B Write and say.

goat   toad   window   elbow

1.
- - - - - - - - - - - - -

2.
- - - - - - - - - - - - -

3.
- - - - - - - - - - - - -

4.
- - - - - - - - - - - - -

 oa ow

A Read and check.

1.

I have a yellow pillow. ☐

I have a yellow bow. ☐

2.

I see a toad. ☐

I see a goat. ☐

3.

It is my elbow. ☐

It is my soap. ☐

4.

It is a boat. ☐

It is a coat. ☐

B Unscramble, write, and say.

1.

d a r o

_____

2.

p s a o

_____

3.

w r o

_____

4.

w p l o i l

_____

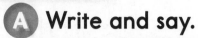

A Write and say.

u e	bl____

B Match.

1.	2.	3.	4.
blue	glue	Tuesday	clue

C Write and say.

1.  b____e

2.  T____ day

3.  g____e

4.  ____ue

long u
ue

A Write and say.

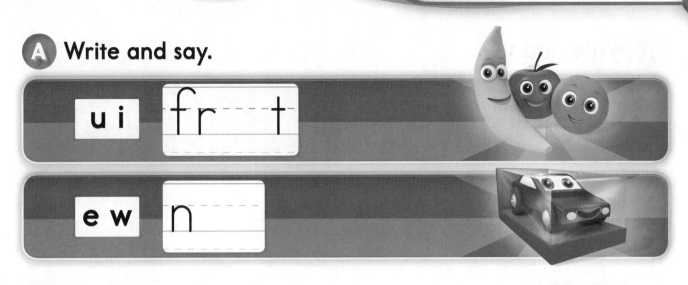

u i fr __ __ t

e w n __ __

B Say and circle.

1.

ui   ew

2.

ow   ui

3.

ew   ow

4.

oa   ew

C Unscramble, write, and say.

1.

w n e

_____

2.

s u t i

_____

3.

w e d

_____

4.

t f i u r

_____

ue ui ew oo

A Write and say.

oo   m _ _ _ n

B Read and check.

1.

It is a zoo. ☐
It is a moon. ☐

2.

I eat food. ☐
I eat fruit. ☐

3.

It is a boot. ☐
It is a zoo. ☐

4.

It is the moon. ☐
It is the boot. ☐

C Write and say.

food   zoo   moon   boot

1.

2.

3.

4.

long u

oo

A Find the words and underline.

njglueahmoonklbootljdewplnewkjsuitlyfruituqfoodtp

B Match.

1.
ue
•

2.
oo
•

3.
ui
•

4.
ew
•

•

•

•

•

C Unscramble, write, and say.

1.

l c u e

_ _ _ _ _ _ _ _ _ _

2.

t f i u r

_ _ _ _ _ _ _ _ _ _

3.

t o b o

_ _ _ _ _ _ _ _ _ _

4.

e d w

_ _ _ _ _ _ _ _ _ _

A Find, circle, and write.

m	o	o	n	z	f
l	c	x	t	u	r
c	p	e	l	l	u
o	e	d	b	k	i
a	t	b	o	u	t
t	s	q	w	o	a

1. _____

2. _____

3. _____

4. _____

B Write and say.

zoo   goat   new   toad

1.  _____

2.  _____

3.  _____

4.  _____

long o   oa   ow

oa ow ue ui ew oo

C Circle the ones that rhyme.

D Do the puzzle.

1.
2.
3.
4.
5.
6.

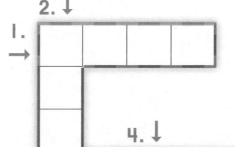
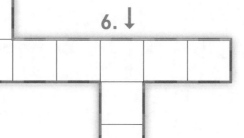

a_e	ame	ake
ate	ave	i_e
ime	ike	ive
ine	o_u	u_e
u_e	ai	ay
ee	ea	y
ey	igh	ie

Open in Colab

y	oa	ow
ue	ui	ew
oo	a	b
c	d	e
f	g	h
i	j	k
l	m	n

o

p

q

r

s

t

u

v

w

x

y

z

These cards
belong to:

_____